DANCING IN THE PRESENCE OF MEN
A Book of Love & Lovers

Joyce Lee

Niambi!
You are dope AF!
I look forward to more

Editors

Melanie Yeyo Carter
www.melanieyeyocarter.com

Cydnee A. Reese
cydneeareese@yahoo.com

Cover Art

Wren Michelle
www.wmsongbirdart.com

Book Layout and Design

Betsy Gomez
ebetsygomez@gmail.com

©2020 Joyce Lee.

All rights reserved. No portion of this publication may be reproduced or transmitted, in any form or by any means, without the express written permission of the author, except for the use of brief quotations in critical reviews.

A note on the typeface: Titles set in Khula by designer Erin McLaughlin. Body set in Adobe Caslon Pro by designer Carol Twombly.

Preface

I can remember the exact moment that I realized I was a writer: East Oakland, California,1990. I was 9 years old, in my room, and angry about something again. I was often silenced as a child because of my blunt and dogmatic analysis of the adults in charge of my life. In my family, children were only permitted to share opinions concerning childish things. My fearless honesty punished me with a familial reputation of being mean-spirited. In efforts to erase that reputation, I often choose journaling my truths instead of speaking them. Subsequently, I grew to prefer solitude over socializing, which was also interpreted as meanness. No matter how well I obeyed, my face showed my discontent. I made every attempt to avoid trouble, and still I could not escape my debauched reputation. I hated being a child. I was regularly shamed for appraising relationships that did not include my complete acceptance. Most of my memories consist of a constant struggle against the delusions of others about me.

I would love to tell you a story of me growing into a full womyn who no longer cares what others think of me. I would love to give you an epic beginning. But I'm afraid that in many ways I am still the same 9-year old, secluded in her bedroom, writing everything I dare not say for fear of the reputation that may follow.

Last year, I watched a docuseries on Netflix entitled *Sex Around the World*. I love sex as a verb and a subject. The docuseries was about the various perceptions of sex in different countries around the world. The subject of sex, no matter where, was always tied to the systematic policing of womyn. The more liberal the country, the more sexually explicit the womyn. In turn, the stricter the laws, the more silent and covered womyn are forced to be. Cisgender, heterosexual men remain more or less the same in every country, unquestioned.

In the docuseries, a womyn in a more conservative country listed some of the many things that womyn dare not do. I was baffled when she said that it was illegal for womyn to dance in the presence of men! I could not relate. It is acceptable, *even encouraged*, for me to twerk in a gentlemen's club or on a television program for men. Actually, it is stereotypically expected that Black womyn know how to *and* love to do overtly sexual dances for others. This world treats me as though my ass-jiggle is my formal greeting!

I grew up in a home and society where I could wear whatever I wanted while always having to cover *something*. Not just physically, but verbally, socially, and emotionally. My complete nakedness was and still is considered rude, and nothing is meaner than a rude Black womyn. I have always received offended responses and been treated as if my isolation is by choice instead of a reaction to rarely being welcomed as I am. Thus, I could completely relate to the womyn in the docuseries in the sense that it is *not* ok for me to dance for myself as if I am my only source of provision. It is considered whorish for me to understand men as adorning garments that I can choose to remove or append at will. I am reputedly conceited if I praise myself for *being* visible without seeking permission or approval.

I am free to dance in the presence of men; however, I have never felt free from judgment while dancing uninhibitedly for myself in the presence of others . . . Consider this book my background music.

"You heard me. You ain't blind."
—Zora Neal Hurston

Hella Old School

Barely *just* connected Jimi's Red House to
a street near East 14th,
just called every ghetto surrounded by cops
Bleaker Street,
just let Break Street break me in,
and here you come talkin' 'bout Tupac!
Damn! These youngstas move fast!
Imma need you to know a Marvin lyric
to the rhythm you'd like to fuck me in.
Take ya time, you at the grown folks table!

And I'm still *just* learning spades and Muddy!
Learning just how nasty Clarence Carter's blind ass was!
Still *just* lettin' Ol' J.T. and Redding give me Stax on
the many ways a strong man can repent—
I'm *just* learning Black Love—
and here you come talkin' 'bout Nas!
I ain't even close, baby!
Spend a little more time on my insides like Wild Bill,
and whisper Bootsie Collins to me.
I need your conversation and vocab to be longer than
an Isaac Hayes and Roy Ayers all night groove
put together.
And don't *eeeeven* expect these learning hips to twerk!

I'm still *just* learning to dance through pain.
Still learning to make love from it!
Still getting used to the snare *pop*,
not bein' a foot stomp 'n' hand clap
that encourages me past the lash 'n' whip!
Still *just* understanding that there is a lovemaking sound
that is all mine!

I'm still caressing in the language of Mayfield,
kissing in Hathaway,
and here you come
talkin' 'bout Wu-Tang Clan!
I ain't even close, baby.
Not even a lil bit.

The Survivor's Guide to Listening

Most of the time
I just remember 'Nita
singing of the same Sweet Love that
the womyn in my family
could never seem to get in return.

Freddy Jackson
meant there was an adult party
and that us kids should stay in our room.
And Jamaica Funk
meant we'd have to wait until their liquor
kicked in really good before coming out.

Johnnie Taylor
meant the womyn were empowered and the house
could be shared equally in celebration of
"Fuck dat Muthafucka!"

Betty Wright
meant I'd only better come out ready to sing along
well enough to give every womyn
in that house hope.
And I usually did.

I knew my mother was in love again when
the house smelled like Clorox, Pine Sol and incense.
I knew things were serious
between her and a new man
when every morning smelled like
crackling sausage, fresh bread and grits.

I could hear how many meals I needed to deny
in the depths of my mother's silence
as she listened
to one of her sister's worries.

If you hang around me long enough,
you will notice that
I have a habit of asking for nothing
and taking up as little space as possible
and cleaning more than I soiled
and apologizing for existing first thing in the morning—
apologizing for interrupting your eyesight.

If you hang around me long enough,
you will notice that
I have a habit of eating
once per day
or less.

Blame my weird nature on my family's welcome.
Blame it on how they put me in the habit of
listenin' and making room for others.

. . . Blues Dancing in Chicago

"The blues swallows all hips, Children.
Conjures 'em into corkscrews and
makes gemstones of muscles in fetid flesh.

Remember You:
deep sorrow and sacrament
exorcising give-a-damn
to the cries of someone else's tortured soul.

Remember You:
suffocated blood and shatter—
apparition pumpin' wet circadian through skin."

An Ode to Johnnie Taylor

I make love like Johnnie:
a crammed righteousness
bona fide enough to
feel slightly slighted and
all the way together.

If a man is with me,
then we may as well be Jheri curled and drinkin'.
Night Train Express, tied up
in fishnet stockings
to a headboard
in a hole-in-the-wall,
fussin' n' fuckin'
in the same four chords,
pleading for understandings,
begging for trust again
and again
'cause my love is just
one gorgeous gotdamn Blues.
Like Johnnie.

Envidiosa

That tall Black American womyn
dancing on the dance floor in Bogotá, Colombia,
she got all these short men in line,
accepting the test of her beauty.

And she so Black,
her smile like a fire in the dark.
It's so beautiful,
it's makin' moths of these men.
And they all in line
hoping she will choose them.
Hoping they will be timely enough
to get a chance at forever with her
and her long, long legs
and her midnight skin
and that bonfire smile she be winkin' with.

I'm sitting here smilin' at the whole scene,
but inside I am jealous.

Not of her height or beauty.
I am shorter than she is.
But I'm still tall for a womyn.
I gotta compensating beauty,
and I am sexy too.
So, I ain't jealous of her gorgeous dance
or the long line of short men
hoping to get a chance at eons with her.

But the hope in her shift 'n' twirl!
The heartbreaking experiences
still light enough for her to only carry on
her tongue and nowhere else in her body!

A body that hasn't been clotted in trauma
but is saturated in wells of
hopeful love—
so much so
she magnetizes possibilities!

Everything in the air around her,
everything she is taking for granted,
I envy.

The Widow

Death has made every day a mystery.
I look forward to wisdom
but have never appreciated
the Humbling and Strengthening Road of Grief that
we all must feel in knowing.

Knowing only knows more ignorance.
I have just met Grief for the first time.
I wish to know her surname—
I wish to track her prints—
I wish to predict her steps—
so that I can be braced and ready when she comes again.

Death has made every day a mystery.

"Today I am wiser
and more in awe of each moment than
I have ever been because I hurt.
Laughter is truly a joy.
I am wiser in pain."

Death, on the other hand,
has made a fool of me.

The Around Far-Gone Nearby
is a virus in all things
and has made a groom of my husband.
They are now a couple,
whom I have the burden of
repeatedly announcing to the world:
"David and Death!"
"Death took David from me!"

I never knew Death had eyes for him
until it was too late!

I wish Death would have compromised and given us
a little more time
like I've seen Death do before.

I wonder what Death said to David.
Did they argue about me as they lay?

I wonder if Grief will visit tomorrow?
She is always soon, on her way,
strong, full of fatigue and apathy,
carrying past packages of present anxieties
together.

We will feel sorrow and know things,
and knowing will make us thirst in ignorance
and we will feel anguish and grow wiser in it.
We will miraculously get through another day that
Death has made a mystery.

Processing the Vortex

The sucky thing about grief is feelings. I gotta either feel the grief or numbness. Every religious person in my family has been offering me Jesus like He's a trending strain of cannabis that I'm oblivious to. I'm drinking way too much because I was drinking too much before the grief, and now the drinking has grief as an excuse. When I don't drink, I sort of feel. I don't feel sad per se. Grief doesn't feel like the sadness I've identified as sadness all of my life. It also doesn't feel like the sadness that others describe when they compare me losing my husband to the loss of their step great-grandmother. I found my husband dead in our home. People seem to want me to *be* sad when I am not. I'm in grief. Grief is so much more permanent. It's a casual, numbing fire. Honestly, when people compare their sadness in losing a pet or step great-grandparent to the grief I feel in losing my younger husband, I really want punch them in the face—left hook! I digress. For me, grief is mostly an uncomfortable indifference.

I can actually feel myself uninterested in. the. whole. fucking. world. I don't give a shit about blue skies or sunny days. Outside, the gorgeous California spring looks like a painted sheet that I usually want to snatch down and use as a blanket to hide under until I die. (What's the point in proceeding with my life when we're all just going to die?) Every minute feels like I'm a kid in a corner being punished, waiting to be set free. Nothing's fun. People are boring. Life is boring. Unless I get high or drunk. My indifference isn't just emotional, it's physical, so I have to overdrink in order to feel drunk. I've done that more times than I care to admit. I'm embarrassing to myself. I drunk-dial exes that I don't even want to be back in a relationship with and curse their current lovers. I'm hurt and volatile towards all of the men who never gave me the love my husband did. I'm mad that I have to live a life with them and my husband had to die. I call current lovers and beg them to come over and touch me, breaking boundaries I've struggled hard to make clear in the past. I drink until I don't hear, see or feel anything that isn't immediately happening right then and there. I hurricane and tornado, and in the morning I'm hungover, and grief is still my covering.

Last night, I called Dwayne. He's a young lover I had in the past until I one day decided it would be best if we kept things strictly platonic. I really don't know what the hell it is that I want from Dwayne. I enjoy looking at him. He's stunning, talented and brilliant, and he knows how to hold space for me in my grief. Not to mention, his penis is gigantic (which is not my thing), but he knows how to take his time with me—or let me take my time with it, rather. When I called Dwayne, I was beyond drunk and had completely forgotten a poem I'd effortlessly said a million times before in front of a crowd of peers. I was embarrassed and wanted the comfort in touch. Dwayne answered his phone in his normal voice, deep and sincere.

"Hello."

"Hey . . . I'm going through some shit, can you come over?"

"I got a gig. I'm in Rockridge. I gotta get on stage in a bit."

"Will you come over after . . . pleeeeeeeeaaase. I don't want anything (I lied), I could just use some company. I'm really . . . I'm not so good right now. I'm really not."

"Hey, Joyce, can I call you back?"

"Sure . . . You know what, no. Don't call me back. I'm so sorry to bother you. This is my shit, not yours. I'm not being fair, I'm manipulating you with my emotions. Listen, try and forget this. You have a good show. Have a groovy night."

"Joyce, no. Stop. No apologies. Listen, just let me call you back."

"No! Okay? . . . *Okay*?!"

". . . Okay."

"Goodnight."

I hung up the phone. Took a shower. Ranted on Facebook. Deleted the rant. Masturbated and went to sleep.

I awoke to my phone ringing and the sun glaring. I answered the phone in a hungover haze. Everything was blurry. I mumbled

"Hello."

"Aye," Dwayne said.

"Hey, how was your show?"

"I'm on my way to you now."

"*Why?!*"

Dwayne hung up.

I got up, slipped on a skirt—fuck panties, they didn't go with my hangover—threw on the first t-shirt I saw laying around. I splashed some water on my face and brushed my teeth. I began drinking water like a castaway. My mind was in a million places. I was still kicking myself for forgetting my poem the night before, berating myself for getting so shamefully drunk, anxious about Dwayne on his way to me, hoping he wasn't angry, hoping I didn't fuck up his mood right before his gig. I wondered if he was coming over just to set boundaries that would prevent me from asking to see him again for a while. Or to personally remove his number from my phone. I walked through the house shaking my head at my own damn self. I was repulsive to me and had no other self to escape to. I figured, I had to take the punches I had thrown the night before. So, I sat on my couch and waited for Dwayne to show up in whatever way he chose.

I saw Dwayne walking from an Uber towards the wooden gate in front. He has a huge afro and carries his electric guitar with him like it's his third arm. He's a long man, around 1.9 meters (6'3"). I'd guess his weight at about 93 kilograms (205 lbs). Dwayne's slender but not thin, just young. He has visible biceps with veins protruding out. The gold rimmed, circle-shaped sunglasses he wore reflected blue against the sun. He smiled when I opened the front door. He gave me a strong, long embrace. I cautiously hugged him back because I was bracing myself for his chastisement. Dwayne took off his shades, placed his electric guitar against the house on the porch, welcomed himself inside, sat on the couch, relaxed, and looked at me carefully.

"How are you, Joyce?"

I lowered my head in complete embarrassment while smiling.

"I'm embarrassed."

"Why?" he chuckled

"Because of everything last night. I'm a mess. I'm so sorry. I'm just my FULL self in this process and—"

"Stop apologizing. Please . . . You really seemed like you were having a hard time last night, and I wish I could've been here for you . . . Joyce, you're such a virtuous person, and your needs have virtue . . . This time and your needs in this time . . . I'm here. I'm here to sit and listen and laugh and do whatever you wanna do ALL day . . . there's absolutely no other place in the world I would rather be. Okay?"

I smiled coyly and looked at Dwayne. "Okay."

"Good!" he laughed "You got any weed?"

Dwayne smoked while I continued to sober and hydrate, and we sat on the front porch drinking lemonade and talking about everything. All of it. His life, his mother, his father, and mine too, for hours. Then we went for tacos in Berkeley and ate and laughed like kings. A friend of Dwayne's called him and wanted to have an impromptu jam session. Dwayne invited me to come with him. I said no thanks and admitted to having perverted thoughts while feeding him a bite of my taco and watching him lick the sour cream from in between the space of his pointing finger and thumb. We both laughed. We went outside, and he hugged me tightly.

"Thank you for being Joyce, Joyce."

I embraced him back. Tightly. I felt the blood running warm and aroused through my entire torso area. I pushed back from the hug and took a few extra small steps backwards. I wanted to fuck him so much.

"Aye, why are you moving away from me? It's all the smoke from the weed, hunh? It's on me?"

I shook my head no like a timid child. Dwayne looked at me confused. I took all the sexual energy I felt, put it in my eyes, and looked at him.

"*Oh!*" he grinned

"Perfect timing, here goes my Lyft!" I said, blushing and rushing into the backseat of the car before Dwayne could have a chance to offer me anything physical. I heard him cackling behind me. I waved at him while riding past. He smiled big and held up his two fingers while placing a joint between his perfect lips.

It was one of my better days.

Talking about Travis . . . and David

While in vigilant search for my shaving razor, which
I envisioned finding:
the spare sharp blades,
wrapped in hard
plastic to protect me
from myself.

I stumbled upon a single earring
that I was certain I had lost
many months ago.

I was so sure it was gone.
I mourned the money spent
on the irreplaceable,
24 karat California rose gold design that
once matched most perfectly with
my wedding ring.

At the immediate absence
of the one missing jewel,
I blamed myself
instead of doing the work
of vigilant searching
for fear of disappointment
in wasting more time
laboring over anything *else*
that could be so easily lost.

So many other earrings
I denied myself
as punishment
for losing one of the pair.

*"I'm not wasting my money
again."*

My grief
would interrupt
the moment
another expensive pair
requested a chance
to be mine too.

All of this time
and nothing was ever lost.

All of the tiny pleasures denied
over blame.
In fear of searching
for something that may hurt
if the time spent seeking it
had only led to seeking.

Interesting
I was more confident
(as though it is my lot in fate)
to search and find
the razor and never the lost jewel.

Online Dating a Black Widow[1]

> *When womyn like me dream of touch apart from obligation,*
> *the world often says "We have place for you, and*
> *we do not care if you cry and yell*
> *because it fits restrained!*
> *We have a name for you,*
> *and you will endure it, like the lingering*
> *scent of your assailant*
> *and the fetters on the boat that snatched you*
> *three worlds away from yourself."*
> —Joyce Lee

My Profile:

"I want 'blah, blah, blah' and someone who I don't have to teach that consensual sex and/or touch is healthy and necessary for humans. I prefer take-charge thinkers who are chill and sane. I'm not a size queen when it comes to penises, but I like them to be big enough so that I can actually feel if one is inside of me. I require much patience. You must understand that I am not looking for a relationship, just touch— but passionate, intelligent touch. What I am asking for is so simple, yet so rarely fully understood."

Reply: I'm just what you need. I'll make sure you are pleased. I am a good listener. I love to please women. I have what you're looking for in penis size. I've attached a couple of pictures. One of my smile and one of my dick.

Me: Niiiiiiice! How about we meet up for a drink to make sure the other is sane and make decisions from there?

---

[1] The female black widow spider is considered the most venomous spider in North America. The venom of the black widow spider is 15 times as toxic as the venom of the prairie rattlesnake. Only the female black widow is dangerous to humans; males and juveniles are harmless. The female black widow will, on occasion, kill and eat the male after mating.

Reply: Okay . . . Or how about we just meet up at my place? I have tons of wine. I'm in the wine industry!

Me: Listen, there needs to be a screening process. I just can't show up to a stranger's house. You could be runnin' snuff films, I'm cool.

Reply: You're totally sane! Just come on over. I don't drive, and I don't feel like riding my bike. We seem like we'd have fun together.

Me: Hey, ass-tit! I know *I'M* sane. What I do not know is if *YOU'RE* sane. Why would *SANE ME* put myself in a position to be in a crazy murdered-online-lookin-for-ass situation? My family ain't gonna understand that shit: me killed fuckin' some random guy online. There *has* to be a screening process. You know what, forget it. There's another guy who just messaged me, and he's willing to meet my basic criteria. Good night, Love.

Reply: Oh :-(I understand. You are a beautiful woman. Well, maybe if you are not vibing with him . . . or, a woman like you sounds like you'll soon be done with him, please consider stopping by. My address is "blah." My phone number is "blah." It is 9pm now. I'll be at home, waiting for you until midnight.

20 Minutes Later, While Standing Outside on His Sidewalk

TEXT: I'm here. But you have to meet me outside and talk first.

He greeted me outside. He lived in a studio apartment that was a part of a huge gentrifying community space from the looks of it. The area felt young and white, and people were roaming inside and outside of the many doors and paths. We strolled around the house while talking about the roses and thorns of online dating. We went up and down stairs that were illuminated by sensory lights, which led to an irradiated path that led to another chill area and community garden in the back of the house.

We sat in the garden and talked until I felt comfortable enough with him to go into his apartment. There were candles everywhere. It was very clean; the bed was made, and he verbally welcomed me. He was civil and heavily accented. "I am Italian and Albanian. I am Koti"

Me: What does Koti mean?
Koti: The young child.
Me: Do you think this is true about you? Are you a young child?
Koti: Well, I *do* have an older sister, and I am the youngest child.
Me: Are you spoiled?
Koti: Not with money, but I was very spoiled with love.

I smiled. I wondered if everything was true: the accent, the safe-seeming invitation, the candlelit studio, his name being Koti.

Me: What made you respond to me online?
Koti: I was bored.
Me: Oh, so that's what the fuck I am, entertainment to you?
Koti: Do you not find me entertaining? I hope you do. I worked hard on a gamble that you would not come. I

hope I am entertaining you as a good host.
Me: Is that accent real?
Koti (laughing): Yes, it's real. I wouldn't know how to fake an accent. I wish I didn't have this one! Would you like a glass of wine?
Me: Sure.

We talked about wine. We talked about travel. He spoke to me in perfect Turkish, only sweet words to which I knew all of the correct replies.

Koti: Ah! You've had a Turkish darling, eh?

I said yes and had another glass of wine.

We made each other laugh. He understood my wit and quickly matched it every time.

Me: I am so sorry for giving you a hard time online. I have needs, but on the other hand I just never know who's on the other side of the screen, and I find it best to be clear and immediately rude if clear isn't enough by itself when dealing with men.
Koti (hunches shoulders): I'm pretty chill.
Me: Yeah, (sips wine) I hope you don't kick me out for sayin' this, but your chill . . . it can easily be misinterpreted as laziness. I mean, I'm making the effort to get up, slip on some clothes, and even lather on a couple layers of my good mascara to meet you for a drink for a simple screening process, and you're too lazy to help yourself get laid? I mean, let's keep it real here, Koti.
Koti: Yeah, well, I thought from your post that someone like you wanted a straight shooter, someone to avoid the lies and bullshit with, yes?

Me: Yes.

Koti: Okay, well the truth was that I didn't feel like going out, but I would be willing to host you in my studio for a romantic night. That's why you're in my studio, with all these candles lit, sipping wine to some chill music. My telling you that I would rather meet here is because I honestly did not feel like going out. I thought we would be perfect together.

Me: So, it doesn't mean that you're just trying to see what you can get away with? Because that's how I see it.

Koti: No. Absolutely no! Due to the rampant disease of rape culture in this country, I can see why this would be your logic, but no. I honestly just did not want to leave my home (looks around). It's a very comfortable place, don't you think?

Me (sips more wine): If we like what happens tonight—and let's keep in mind, we might *not* like what's about to happen, we don't know our chemistry until we're *in it*, ya know? But if we like what's about to happen, how often would you be willing to meet up?

Koti: My schedule is actually crazy. Maybe like once a week?

Me, looking Koti dead in his eyes: When was the last time you had sex?

Koti: About 3 months.

Me: Do you miss it?

Koti (suddenly serious): Yes. Yes, I do.

Me (smiles deviously): Isn't that why you reached out to me? Not just because you were bored but because you miss sexual touch?

Koti (grins): Yes.

Me: No, fully admit it.

Koti: Yes. I responded to your profile because I miss sexual touch (reservedly grinning).

Me: I need you to remember that the whole way through this okay? You and I, we both just need touch. I miss touch. I miss connecting passionately and someone else being in charge of how big my orgasms are. I miss skin in between my teeth and being wet on a man's breath. I am used to having sexual outlets, and I am used to having them on my terms—well, with the exception of this situation. You wouldn't budge on meeting for drinks, but you continued being kind after I called you an ass-tit (laughs).
Koti (laughing): I was just being honest.

I arose from my chair and sat on Koti's bed, and he immediately joined me. We almost kissed until:

Me: Wait. Do you have any active cold sores or tares or bumps in your mouth, because if so, it's totally fine to not kiss me? I'm sorry if the talk of STDs is killing the mood, but I have never had an STD or anything, and I just want to keep it that way.
Koti (opening his mouth and letting me inspect): No. No, I do not get sores or bumps on my lips. It's totally fine. It's good to check in. That's healthy.

We kissed. Kissing led to me laying down, and Koti uncovering my right nipple and sucking on it while playing it between his teeth and his tongue. His fingers slid under my dress and up my inner thigh as my legs opened wider and wider until his fingertips found their way to my pantiless, freshly waxed and dripping labia. Koti played with my exposed vulva, and his touch felt like we had known each other for years. I moaned and he worked his fingers in and out of me like he had perfected my orgasm with other womyn in the backseats of cars during high school.

Koti held open my right leg while I rubbed his dick and balls over his thin pajama pants. He took off his shirt. His chest was small and he had a cute belly. We rubbed each other while staring intentionally into the other's eyes and smiling, unashamed.

Me: How tall are you?
Koti: I'm 5'8".
Me: How do you feel about that?
Koti (smiling): Well, for America, it is short. But I feel just fine.
Me: For America, it is average. 5'8" / 5'9" is the average height of a man.
Koti: How tall are you?
Me: 5'9".

Koti began kissing my neck and cradled my opened knees on his elbows. He played with my legs, positioning while looking down at my wetness. He teased an entry into my vagina with the tip of his middle finger and then ring finger and got her so wet that by the time he added his pinky finger, I was screaming in orgasm.

Koti's dick was rock hard. He put on a condom and fucked me, hard and passionately. I had already cum during the fingering, and the penetration prolonged the body high of my orgasm. Koti suddenly stopped and sat up. "Did you cum?! Because I'm about to cum so fucking hard, did you cum? You're so wet, I can't tell." Nodding yes, I pointed at him "You lost your accent," I teased. Koti broke out in laughter. "You are hilarious!" He resumed, inside of me.

Koti's flesh felt restorative on top of mine. His hips grinding in perfect circles, and deep thrusts had my entire vagina applauding. My hips were going up, down, and counterclockwise in sync with the rhythm of his thrusts and circles. My hands squeezed his ass, and it clinched as I pushed him deeper inside of me. I licked his neck sloppily and massaged his scalp and the back of his neck while his thrusts and rhythms grew more intense. My hands caressed and traveled back and forth from his body, scalp, and clinched ass as we kissed. "Awwww!! I'm cumming!" Koti moaned before burying his face in the pillow below my head and screaming into it as his entire body shivered. He continued in minor convulsions until our rhythm simmered, slowed, and stopped completely.

Koti (still moaning from the sex while walking towards the kitchen to get a paper towel to wrap the used condom in): Do you need a paper towel? Or better yet, the bathroom is there, and there are some moist wipes near the toilet.

I grinned. I jumped up with a renewed liveliness and cleaned myself in the bathroom.

Koti came into the bathroom when I was finished, and while he was urinating and moaning from the ticklish sensation, I was calling an Uber.

He came outside of the bathroom to find me fully dressed.

Koti: You're dressed?!
Me: Yes, and I've called an Uber. It's on the way . . . I really enjoyed myself.

Koti (looking confused): Me, too. That's why I thought you'd stay a bit longer.
Me: No. Not a good plan for me. Just touch, remember? But you know, I'll get with you . . . once a week you said, right?
Koti (looking confused and a little robbed at the sight of my hand already on the front doorknob): I mean, yah. But honestly, I really, really enjoyed you. I mean, I enjoyed your company—like you are real from beginning to end . . . You can just lay a bit? . . . Ok, you're right, you were clear . . . So, anytime really! We can get together any time, not just once a week!

His echo chased into the night behind me.

Lost in Translation

Translation is everything.
Trust or bust
is always in the translation.

He asks what I need
with his dick in his smile's hand,
and I only share my body
with humans
who see me as human.

His entitlement translates
my every word to mean sex
with him
immediately.

All of a sudden
he refers to me in pieces
that exist for his pleasure only.

Each part of my body
he cites
is dissected and detached
at the dining table before us
and self-served over drinks.
He even calls
my look of thorough and utter disgust—
my obvious silent boil—
sexy.

He has translated himself into
Lower Than Nothing and Is.

Too fool to feel
the atmosphere
mutating him into
Nothing *More*.

Part of a Conversation About Feminism With an Extremely Sexy, Devout, Muslim Boxer I Am Teaching Online English to

Him: Men have needed womyn to help them. Since the garden, it has been this way. Womyn were born fully equipped. Man was born needing her and not knowing it—even in the garden. Man says womyn are weaker because she came from his rib, but no holy scripture of any religion speaks of why, how, or what her need was for the rib—what did she use it for?! Holy scripture says we are *all* made of and will return to the dust of the ground! So, *maybe* the rib was a simple sacrifice for the man?

No intelligent human being would give her all without requesting some sort of sacrifice in return. Maybe the rib represents man's most mediocre effort in exchange for the eternal help we need because we are stupid! Haha! When we first become men, we are no different than a toddler's imagination. We hold a fantasy of what a boy always thought a man should be, and we live too fast! Most womyn's focus is usually on living well, not fast.

This is why every man, no matter the gender or sexuality, needs a womyn in his life—this is why men *need* womyn.

Me: To keep y'all from killin' your simple ass selves?

Him (laughs hysterically until tears): Most of us . . . YES!

Me *(thinking, "I wanna fuck you SO fucking much!")*, straight-faced: Hmmm! I enjoy your point of view. Very good on explaining yourself. Next subject.

All That Smiling

His clothes
were always as clean as
the house, as together as
the kids, as good as
the meals, and as strong as
the prayers . . . as sincere as
the smile that greeted him
at the front door every night,
adorned
in new negligees as fragile as
his ego, as thick as
my will to be
a really good womyn to him,
only him . . .

And he translated my love language
into my slavery . . .

I did ALL that smiling
only to beg 'n' frown.

Untitled

*"If you are willing to suddenly compromise your things and space,
you just might be in Love.
If you are willing to compromise your morals and personal happiness,
you are definitely in Hell."
—Joyce Lee*

When I see a young womyn
in love and arguing
with her beloved—
her eyebrows furrowed,
lips cinched—
her solution: anything but leave.

I become desirous.

I wish
my forgiveness was young.

Wish I had hope in men.

I wish
that hopefulness excited me
to groom to perfection.
To laugh for his laughter.
To smile to ease his insecurities.

Instead, my hope in men
is grey and bedridden,
and my forgiveness
is cremated ashes
on a shelf in my father's house
that I have yet to face.

One mistake will cost you me.

I wish I cared enough to argue.

I wish my love had that much Life.

Your Love

When we met
you were a rescue
to my life of fatigue,
and you said loved me.

You loved me
through the grief of my abandonment.
I felt I owed you the Earth.
So, I gave you my hand in marriage
and children with potential
to the ethers.

In an effort
to say, "thank you,"
in an endeavor
to say, "I love you, too,"
I endure your bullying family
you love.

The overbearing religion
you love.

The curt rage you apologize for, but
you love.

To say, "I love you,"
I obligate myself to give
you good kisses and head
in truce after every argument.

I martyr my soul,
reassure myself that you don't mean the meanness,
recap your apologies,
recount the children we've raised,
retell the number of anniversaries we celebrate.

I repeat.
Staying . . .

Even after the first
and second time
you hit me.

The Monster's Monster

Nature was questioned,
then God,
but first Self.

Then I was made
in your image:

Four limbs
from earth's
four corners.

I was human,
and you did not know
yourself.

You created me,
a Beast of Labor.
Cut deep
and stitched me,
pointed at my scars,
named them Flaws.

Called yourself a genius
and kind and creative,
yet you could never figure
what to call me—
not even Yours,
never Mine.

Monster.

You made a monster
in *your* image!
Of all the possibilities
of things to make!

You made a monster.

So that you could
fear until hate
and hate until death
and die running from
what *you* alone created.
And I cried over you until
I died too.

And love had nothing
to do with it.

I cried for separate identity.

I always knew
your eyes, the most powerful
eyes to ever see me,
were not my own.

I always knew
I had another name so beautiful
and would never know it.

I always knew
I was human.

I always knew
my name is not,
never was, nor will ever be
Frankenstein . . .

That name is
and always will be
yours.

Flips the Script

(Written for Snap Judgment LIVE)

Floyd! Floyd was a very sweet boy I knew in jr. high school. I have purposely blocked out a lot of jr. high, but I remember Floyd because Floyd was the first boy who I knew for a *fact* was head over heels in love with me. I could always tell where Floyd sat in every class because "I love Joyce" was carved into each of his desks, and every time I looked up, I would catch Floyd staring at me. I wasn't sure how I felt about Floyd. I just knew that he loved me, and it felt good to be loved.

Once, Floyd and the class clown Gerald got into an argument in front of the entire class, and Gerald blurted out "If you so big 'n' bad why don't you tell Joyce you love her?! You'dun carved her name on everything 'cept yo forehead!" The entire class laughed. I looked at Floyd. And even though I couldn't see his eyes through his thick coke bottle glasses, and through *my* thick coke bottle glasses, I could sense his shyness as he lowered his head and said nothing.

That day, when I returned home from school, my mother was in the kitchen preparing dinner. I rushed to tell her everything about Floyd in excitement: how Floyd loved me and everyone knew! How awesome it made me feel to be loved—how withdrawn Floyd became when Gerald exposed him, and how I saw Floyd's quietness as an opportunity to ask him to the jr. high winter formal dance—

"Wait, wait, wait! Run that by me again little girl, you plan on doing what?!"

I knew that I had said something wrong but had no idea what it was, and my mother was looking at me so seriously.

"What are you going do? Say what you're going to do again."

"Imma ask Floyd—"

"You ain't askin no man but Jesus for *nuthin*! YOU are the gift! You stay wrapped in beauty, and say nothing! You do not choose boys, boys choose you! Do you understand me?"

I trusted my mother's advice about attraction because my mother was always the most beautiful mother in the room. Always! When I was in the 6th grade, there was this *gorgeous* teacher named Mr. Randall who only had eyes for my mother. Mr. Randall was the sweetest and most fun teacher in Oakland! All of my friends *and* their mommas had a crush on Mr. Randall, but every day, without fail, Mr. Randall would stop *me* in the halls to ask, "How's your mother?"

One hot day, at the beginning of class, Mr. Randall questioned me about my mother, and I told him that she had taken the day off of work. Mr. Randall's eyes lit up. He turned to the class and said, "Lawd, it's hot! Who wants ice cream?!" The class cheered. Mr. Randall walked us around the corner to the store near my house and bought us all ice cream. We took the route passing my house on the way back to the school. Mr. Randall stopped in front of my house and looked at me. "Hey, Joyce, you wanna go in and check on your mother?" I went inside and told my mother that the entire class was outside and that Mr. Randall bought us ice cream. She, of course, came outside and said hello to Mr. Randall. And he, of course, said hello to my mother while turning a bright red. But nothing ever happened between my mother and Mr. Randall because even though my mother was wrapped in gorgeous with an afro on top, Mr. Randall never asked her out. But James did.

James was my mother's boyfriend. When James first met my mother, he was always praising her beauty. James bought my mother fur coats, jewels, two Mercedes-Benzes, a four-bedroom house, and he'd take us all on weekend outings.

As years passed, James's criticisms of my mother became much more frequent than his compliments. My mother and us were financially well kept with James, so she allowed him more say, and then more say, and then after a while it became a silent law that my sisters and I weren't allowed to do anything or go any place that James didn't approve of. As more time passed, neither could my mother.

James always invited himself into every conversation involving my mother, and he'd heard me telling her about Floyd. "Yeah you the gift, you see! Don't be stupid! You ain't desperate and ugly like some of your friends you bring 'round here, what that girl's name? The one you brought 'round here yesterday? Yeah, her! Lawd! She ain't got no help coming! Now, she gon' have to beg a man for attention! Don't act like you got them problems. *You* talk too much, and men don't like that. But you're still pretty enough to choose! Men *choose* you, you hear?"

I became so excited at the idea that of all of the beautiful girls at school, someone would choose me! I fantasized daily that a sweet and shy boy of my dreams (with the psychic ability to know that I had a crush on him) would be so overwhelmed at the gift of my beauty that he'd make a huge scene in front of the entire school just to ask me out!

You know . . . no one ever really asked me out most of high school. I was this sassy boyish church girl thespian who loved the Blues. So, I waited . . . And waited . . . Freshman year—nothing. Sophomore year, I had a crush on my best friend Tyler, but he never asked me out— Tyler chose every girl except for me! When I finally began dating, I was so grateful *just* to be considered that I said yes to every single guy who asked me out!

There was Jaden, who took me out on one romantic first date and then demanded that I pay for all of his school lunches since we were "together." Fred complimented me in private but had another girl with a "better body" who he preferred to be seen with in public. Jace . . . I pretty much never saw Jace because he was always fighting and getting suspended from school. But they all thought I was beautiful enough to choose!

This is how I dated. Yes after yes, year after year, man after man, until I was around 25 years old. I knew I had a pattern of dating the wrong men, but I could not pinpoint why . . . until I took a trip back home to visit my mother.

She had not been feeling her best, so I suggested we stop by the hospital and get her a quick check-up before going on our planned spa day. James met us at the hospital, and he looked a little worried about my mother's health but seemed more concerned with her being an ear to his personal mulling. Without thought for permission of any kind, James rambled while following my mother into her examination room. And all of a sudden, in the middle of her getting her check-up, at the age of 46, my mother had a stroke.

A nurse came to the waiting room to alert me. I truly believed the nurse was mistaken until she took me only a few steps behind a door, where I saw a bunch of folks in blue working heartily on my mother. She looked so helpless with tubes sticking out of her from everywhere. And James . . . I saw James standing *over* my mother . . .

"Take off all your jewelry and give it to me so I can keep it. I spent a lot of money on this stuff to let the folks in here steal it."

I thought I was in a nightmare until the nurse addressed me. "Ma'am, we're going to keep your mother here with us for a few days. How about you drive home and pick her up some clothes?"

The room was spinning. My legs felt like two heavy sinking ships. I turned around and exited the room. I didn't notice the halls my feet were dragging through or the other patients in the waiting room or the sliding doors as I exited the hospital. Nothing else mattered. I wouldn't have noticed the time of day had it not been so hot. The sun scorched me back to reality.

I took a few deep breaths. I dug in my purse for keys as I walked to my mother's car and heard, "Ay! Aaay! Aaaaay,

Thickums! You fine as fuck gworl! Ay, come here, lemme holla atchu for a minute!" I was annoyed and a little afraid, but I smiled, said thank you, and got into the car. For the entire ride, from and back to the hospital, I interrogated every discussion and gesture of my mother's that I could remember. I needed to make sense of why she was in that hospital bed! It was inexplicable to me why a womyn so resilient and forthright wouldn't tell James to stay in the waiting room with me while she got her check-up, or to shut up about the jewelry! I also wondered why that fool in the parking lot would think *any* womyn coming fresh out of a hospital is in the mood to be cat-called?! Why didn't *I* tell *him* to shut up?! Why did I say thank you?!

I re-entered the hospital in a worried march only to see James on his way out.

"Wait, you're leaving? You're not even going to stay an *hour*?!"

"I got some business I need to take care of. It's a good thing your mother has you here. I'll be back when I can."

I sat next to my mother, staring at her IV and getting comfortable in the chair that would be my bed for the next four days. James never returned to the hospital that day, and the beeping of my mother's heart monitor was the only sound in the room. Time didn't exist anymore. All I could do was study this amazing womyn who'd known me longer than anyone else in the world and had taught me everything I'd known. I caressed my mother's hand gently.

"Mom, do you want to die here? This way, *waiting*? Waiting for this man to be everything you deserve? Waiting for him to become what *you* have always wanted? Waiting for him to *choose* **you**?"

I'd never spoken to my mother like we were just two womyn before. I expected her to grow suddenly defensive and put me in a child's place. But she let my words have their way in her ears. She stared at the ceiling. A single silent tear rolled down the side of her face. And then I said the only thing my memory could connect to that moment.

"Momma . . . you should've let me ask Floyd to that dance! I'm so serious, momma. You should've asked out Mr. Randall, and you should've let me ask Floyd to the winter formal dance when I was in jr. high! They chose us so genuinely that they feared us! I know Mr. Randall's gorgeous self would at least be *here* by your side and not anywhere else! Floyd would be here too! Thick coke bottle glasses and all!"

She laughed until I couldn't resist laughing with her.

It took time for my mother to heal but as soon as she did, she left James . . . and dated her share of charming disasters since! But also since, my mother has been my hero and example about the power of choice because nowadays, *she always chooses herself*, <u>first</u>.

Reflection in Return

(GAORI/ Maradua, Colombia 2019)

There's one other Black womyn in this jungle with me.
She's older than me.
Her eye roll when I say hello is about my father's age.
The way she sucks her teeth at my smile
come from some West Indian island, mid-colonization.

But I'm new to her, though.
'Cause I keep in mind that she's me—
she's the part of me that don't love me
for no good reason.
So, I dress pretty every day for her
and smile and say hello
with my whole heart.
I won't let her offend or ignore her own mirror!
I stay in her face, smiling sincere beauty and love.
No matter what I look like, I think of me.
I know, even if she forgot,
we all we got in this jungle.

Today, I wore a thin and flowing dress,
oiled my Black skin to a shiny marble,
matched eyeshadow with headscarf with stained lipstick.

"¡Que linda!" She smiled,
telling me how beautiful my scarf is.
Finally giving me a chance to praise my own
reflection in return.

Sweet Talker

He said, "You know there isn't a thing that I don't notice about you, right? Everything about you is carved into my brain. I notice how you're always there for people, not only close friends, but almost *anyone* who *needs* you—that's why you don't have much time to be there for *everyone* who just *wants* you around. You give all of yourself to a few people at a time, but that's a lot of people the way you give. You're so warm, but you're not nice on purpose. The first couple of things you show people are your small, smiling teeth and your deadly, loud bite. Not because you want to seem tough. You know your own spirit, and you know others know it too, even before they know *you* well. But you want them to know that you can and will hurt to protect. It's like you show people your bite to protect them from it. And you're never completely still. A part of you is always moving, shaking. It shows your naturally anxious thought pattern. Even now, while you're cooking for me: a man who everyone else has thrown away because throwing me away is the trend this month. Here you are, offering me your time and a meal because you know I am *in need* of a friend. But you're making me a meal you haven't once stopped moving for. You keep stirring, adding spices, love and care to what you are feeding me. When your hands stop mixing, chopping and pouring, your thigh muscles contract, wiggling your waist and ass, and I know that's not a respectful thing to mention, but I'd have to be dead not to notice, and I'm just sayin', I notice you."

"I can only imagine what a fierce womyn like you has added to herself. The love and care . . . The seasonings, the flavors and fire . . . I know this kind of honest flattery makes you want to run out of this kitchen, maybe even out of your own skin. I can tell from your uncomfortable smile and silence. But . . . I'm imagining how *you* taste . . . I bet, even with all of your zest . . . I bet you taste so sweet."

One Day Out of Nowhere

I do not remember the day
my intuition was born,
just the pull and wrestle
against my mother's guidance,
and it's worried nails sinking into my flesh,
her frantic and wild eyes
in response to my every "No!"

I severed her opinion's tongue
with care and something candid
only to tie it in a box and bow
so it could be only hers again
to guide another . . . or bury.

My mother is a good mother.
One day, out of nowhere,
she raised a womyn,
and since then
I have been determined
to make my own mistakes.

. . . In Harlem . . .

"I'm glad you could make it over."

I smile. He smiles more brightly.

"You know it's crazy that we are meeting in New York . . . I'm so glad. You have no idea what it means to me just to see a familiar face."

I take off my coat and shoes.

"Oh. Well, you know you don't really have to do that, but I appreciate the gesture. Let me show you around. Ok, here is the living room—of course this is the hallway. To the left is the kitchen, and if you can believe it or not, I've been cooking *hummha*! Uhm, you're welcome to anything in here by the way."

I nod.

I take off my belt and pants.

He points.

"*Uuuuh*. Over there is the bathroom."

I take off my shirt.

"Would you like to go to my bedroom?"

I take off my bra.

He grabs me and kisses my neck and my shoulders. Cups my breast and bites my nipples. He kneels.

Squeezes my behind and kisses my thigh, licks my tattoo, pulls my panties to my ankles, buries his face in my vulva. My hands remain on my hips, and his are wherever they roam. He is moaning and slurping, and he feels good. He pauses everything to hold my naked body tight. He is hunched and fully clothed, and I am the most important person in the world right now.

"It's been so long. You have no idea how good you feel. I'm so starved—"

"Take off your clothes and take me to your room," I interrupt.

He springs up. Undresses as he walks. I sprawl wide across his bed and relax in a comfortable position on my belly. He grabs the sealed condom box. I need to see that the box was sealed and brand new. He knows this. I see. I smile and nod yes.

I am his for now with every light on in the apartment
and the window open
and the conversation in the streets
and the politicians on the television.

"Look at me."

I roll over on my back as he climbs in between my legs. He is big. He needs to see my face as he tastes me. He needs to know for sure when I'm ready for him to enter. I feel his warm tongue until I cannot tell his wet from mine. I whimper consent. We share eyes. He slides into me and goes somewhere where he is rich and born with wings. I can hardly take him. I waiver between moans and grunts, and he is rich and flying, and I am cumming and wincing and gripping a fistful of his hair. He slows and pulls out of me.

"I need to calm down. I need this to last. I'm honestly in this for the connection . . . I've missed your touch."

I turn back onto my belly while he is speaking. He bites my ear, kisses the side of my neck. I forward my knees into a childlike squat and clinch onto the headboard. He enters me again. Twelve seconds later, he is louder than every light on in the apartment
and every open window
and the conversation in the streets
and the politicians on the television,
and he shoves himself in so deep I let out a wail. He pushes in more. Pushes deeper and deeper until he quivers. His entire body relaxes with our next exhale. He pulls himself out of me. Slowly. Kisses me from spine-top to ass.

I get up. I go to the bathroom and shower. I go to the kitchen, and he is wearing sweatpants and holding two cups of tea.

"No thanks." I smile, put on my panties, my bra.

"Yeah, I found everything just fine. The apartment is really nice, even bigger than the house in Berkeley. I didn't know that was possible in New York."

I put on my jeans and belt.

"No thanks. I'm not hungry. Don't bother. Besides, you got enough to focus on, I've heard about Columbia's graduate programs. Imma get outta your hair."

I smile big. Put on my shirt and walk towards the front door. Put on my shoes.

He blocks the door. He speaks of schedules and time and future possibilities. He speaks in Threeyearsago. He wants.

"I don't have it anymore. I did when you met me. It dangled in my earrings and giggled with me remember? I waved it over your face like a carrot, and you played the ass for it a time or two, remember? And it's not that you don't deserve it. I'm not saying that you don't or do. I'm saying that it's gone. I gave it away about eight months ago. He has frostbite for a grip, but it didn't stop him from taking it. I think I saw it once in his bathroom, on a high shelf above his toilet, caged under an upside-down wine glass right next to a pulled wisdom tooth. I'm sure it's still there collecting dust. He *would* keep it in a place easy to forget. You will have to go to his house to get it. But be ready to kill and die when you come to his door. He is very protective. I think that's why I gave it to him. So, I'd know for sure it would be extra safe."

I put on my coat.

He stepped to the side as I left.

Dressed for Dinner

Making Love to a man feels different.
There is much worry
      because there is nothing to worry about with him.

The mother in me becomes panicked,
afraid she might die if her hands
do not soon find familiar
cries to fix a man-child who needs
cleaning or changing.

This man has mothered himself, and
I do not know what to do with my hands.
I stand bare in discomfort while in my dinner dress.

He circles me like gold trimming
on Jihong porcelain,
his gaze renders me a living feast.

I stand taut, secretly yearning to
instigate my own devouring.
I resent my trembling and loathe realizing
this is who I am when
I am with a man who needs no mothering:
panicking prey.

His orbiting completes behind me.
He groups my free-flowing hair and
positions it over my shoulder.
His lips graze my exposed neck.
His fingers play harp with the texture of my dress.
"Tell me," he whispers,
"What do you have on under this dress?"

"Nothing," the girl says.

He unzipped me.

I stood stunned at the sound of my own innocence.

Love Anyway

I do not know you,
but let me Love you anyway.

You do not have to trust my intentions to
believe my avowal.
No nuptial is needed to submit unreservedly to
my touch.

Please allow me devotion.
I must extol, Love.
I ache to alleviate,
and would Love to
greet you in every attempt to make Love.

When your fingers scuttled
half of a crucifix across your chest,
as you commanded "lick,"
I grew 10,000 happy tongues,
and my soul leapt, longing for
more instructions, for
more blessings
I can give!
I do!

What I do not have, I will find here,
at the altar of your body!
Allow me worship!
Let me say "Love!"
Let you not run!
Let us ignore all suffering
which begot us
into this now sanctified vulnerable!

Let us lick sweat into wine!
Let us feed our 5,000 busted and famished cores
with two bodies and five senses
that boldly touch and agree!

Salvation has no respect of history!
Heaven does not withhold for genealogy's sake!
Consequently, I do not have to know you to say "Love!"
Just as Love requires no decree to make Itself!
Allow me to make Love to you!

Allow my tongue to circle
around your power for
six days and roar on the seventh!
Let us witness the falling of
miraculous fortifications!

Allow me to make you
ritual and testimony
of what Love can be and do
when we bend for Its sovereignty,
when we resist and escape all laws and tradition,
when we become miracles wrapped in flesh and
not expectations,
when we are both
parched wells *and* jaws of asses!
Let us allow Love to be used and use us!
Trust!

We will *not* die,
but be taken up suddenly
by whirlwind!

And the wise will follow
the most exceptional supernova,
across the worst conditions,
in search of our temporary yet
Eternal Truth.

Luke 12:34

"For where your treasure is, there your heart will be also."

Once and Forever:
There was a boy I met in college. We were both heartbroken. I was newly divorced and scarred, and he was a set of blue owl eyes in a dark rowdy bar in Jamestown, North Dakota. Eyes that melded into my flesh and every step. The one dimming stage light and his blonde were the only electricity in the room. He walked to me in spellbinding pull. I stood in guarded fear of his whiteness.

"I do not know why I believe I should worship you, but I do and will," he actioned throughout the night. We made love and made more when we stuck around to heal one another's wounds. We made more love.

"I am leaving now, but I am always here." I proved through long distance phone calls and texts for several years to North Dakota.

We made love over the phone, through holidays and relationships and break-ups and new jobs and purchased homes and occasional vacations to see the other. We made love through baby-fame and pro Black/anti white supremacy campaigns. We made love while loving other people, while losing ourselves. We encouraged each other in authenticity and personal freedom while continuing to make good love.

There is this house in Fargo, North Dakota. A very special someone with eyes like an owl, which still shine bright blue in the dark, lives in it. He is beautiful, fit, and a full-grown man now. His house has an upstairs, a downstairs, three rooms, a basement, and a water heater he put in with his own hands. He has a motorbike, a trampoline, a dirt bike, a snowboard, a skateboard, a hunting rifle, a military badge, a black belt in martial arts, and room for me. No matter what, he always keeps so much room for me.

Love's Gratitude

(After taking ayahuasca in the Colombian mountains)

If ever there was Love
and not the will for
someone outside of ourselves to
yield like a dog to sounds of
our impromptu commands.

If ever there was Love and depth
instead of debts in
the guilt trips of Memory Lane
and insecure insecurities
and the neediness in doubt.

If the Love is real,
joy cannot exist amid
another's captivity.

If the Love is honest,
the observation of
another's trapped eyes—
the quiet of
a partner's tyrannized tongue—
will and should humiliate us.

Love is FREE
and costs us all
our selfishness and
stunted growth and
willful ignorance.
Love costs
our old traditions and ways.

Love costs complete obedience and
loyalty to IT!
Love is power without ego.

If we want Love,
we must trust Its sovereignty!
Trust Love to stay for as long as
it is welcomed to be Free!

Love does not exist to eternally serve and
salve our personal feelings.

I declare my Only Truth:
Love Is and Does!

I have only heard two stories of Love:

1) He/They/She introduces and all is joy.
2) He/They/She exits and all is sorrow.

Love has taught me to consider both in gratitude.
Oh, how grateful I am for Love's comings and goings!

To have witnessed Its steps in my home.
To have made Love to Love! Have Love hold me until
It watched me sleep and
sang of my beauty in the morning!
What a blessing to argue and
fight with and for Love many a late night!
To have it protect me!
How rich I am to partake in the forgiveness of Love!
To be corrected humble by it!
To know Love enough to be Its faithful advocate!

How grateful I am in Love's going!

My sorrow is mine and mine alone!
Love is Free from sorrow and
bends to its own will—always!
I am grateful to learn Freedom
by way of Love's Freedom!
Even if it means my transitory confusion,
even at the expense of my hurt feelings.

Credit: Russellreno Photography

About the Author

Joyce Lee is an international storyteller and performance poet. Her performances of her own creative nonfiction constantly receive standing ovations and encores from fans and personal heroes.

Joyce Lee is an explorer of emotional and physical life. She travels the world and writes, but she is not a travel writer. Instead, each place she wanders, each country, is allotted by her to introduce its own spirit. Joyce listens to that spirit and takes notes. Sometimes the note is a memory, sometimes a story, but every time a poetic gift to her audience. She currently resides in Bogotá, Colombia, with plans to continue her travels in 2020 to complete her first novel.

If you would like to be a financial contributor to Joyce's artistic process, you can be charitable at paypal.me/Joyce509, and if you would like to connect with Joyce, you can find her on Instagram (@fuss_boxx) or join her Facebook fan page, Joyce Unspeakable Joyce (https://www.facebook.com/Joyce-Unspeakable-Joyce-150669241682991/). Lastly, if you are interested in purchasing other works by Joyce, you can find her first published book of poems, *My Soul Is a Witness* (Bootstraps Press, 2017), at www.spdbook.org, and you can download Joyce's album of poems, *No Country for Honest Womyn*, at www.joycelee.bandcamp.com

Accolades

Joyce Lee has a B.A. in English with a concentration in writing and a minor in Public Relations from Jamestown University.

Joyce Lee is and has been:

The 2009 and 2010 Oakland Grand Slam Champion • The 2014 Ill List Champion • A storyteller for WNYC's Snap Judgment LIVE *since 2010 • A guest storyteller at Third Coast Review in Chicago, Illinois • A guest storyteller at Stanford University • A featured poet in Season 3 of TVOne's* Lexus Verses & Flow *• The featured poet for 2018 GIA Conference in Oakland, California • A guest panelist at UC Berkeley's Artist and Activism panel • The featured poet at US-FCA's Honoring Malcolm X • The guest speaker at University of the Pacific on "The Importance of Art in Society" • A guest speaker at UC Berkeley's Ethnic Studies department • A featured poet at UC Berkeley's Women of Color Conference • The featured poet and writing workshop facilitator for #Colored2017 in Tacoma, Washington, as well as #Colored2017 in Arima, Trinidad • A volunteer and the featured poet for the first annual Black History Month Slam in Hamburg, Germany (2018) • A volunteer and facilitator of a monthly writing workshop and open mic in Medellín, Colombia • A volunteer, facilitator and host of a monthly writing workshop and open mic in Bogotá, Colombia, through Paradox & Poetry*

Made in the USA
Monee, IL
18 August 2020